The Others:
A Guide to Conscious Thinking

By: Lion's Den

Table of Contents

Introduction	…………………………………………………………………………	**Page 2**
Chapter 1	The Others: Who Are They, Exactly? ……………………………	**Page 3**
Chapter 2	Perception …………………………………………………………	**Page 6**
Chapter 3	Inner Turmoil ………………………………………………………	**Page 9**
Chapter 4	Relationships ………………………………………………………	**Page 12**
Chapter 5	Social Settings ……………………………………………………	**Page 16**
Chapter 6	Conflict ……………………………………………………………	**Page 19**
Chapter 7	Aspirations & Motivation …………………………………………	**Page 22**
Chapter 8	Creativity …………………………………………………………	**Page 25**
Chapter 9	Humanitarian Endeavors …………………………………………	**Page 28**
Chapter 10	Spirituality …………………………………………………………	**Page 31**
Chapter 11	Self-Awareness ……………………………………………………	**Page 34**

Introduction

What is wisdom? There are those who look to wisdom as a conceptual virtue acquired through past experiences. Then there are those who see it as the byproduct of connecting with a Higher Source for answers to some of life's greatest problems. Some may say that wisdom is a combination of both of these, and an overall knowledge of the natural world from learning from exterior sources. While all responses to the inquiry of wisdom are correct, the most precise answer goes to those who opt out of commonality.

In the uncommon response, there is no bias, preference, or one-sided approach to the definition of wisdom. It is open ended, unclassified and not generalized. It is not good, bad, or stuck on what wisdom is versus what it isn't. It simply gives an umbrella perspective of all of the things that wisdom can possibly be. Beyond the simple question of what wisdom is, those who opt out of commonality challenge us to look at life this way, in its entirety.

Uncommon individuals believe in going against the grain in all areas of life. While we may never know their answer to the proposed question, they would encourage us to look a little deeper. As opposed to focusing on a right versus wrong type of response, they would want us to analyze their acknowledgement and pursuit of the gray area, which presents the possibility of the less common, or unbiased response. The uncommon belief is that in life, we don't always have to choose the socially acceptable or preferred way of a thing, whether it be an answer, a path, or even a way of living. They inspire us to understand that it is okay, in some instances, to consider all perspectives, all options and all possible solutions towards anything we face in our lives.

Uncommon individuals don't believe in the word, "one-sided." They believe in open ended perspectives. They are more inclined to stick with variables as opposed to constants and they greatly value the ideas of changing methods based on the evolution of personal thought processes. They don't fall into the temptation of "choosing" this or that because their standpoints are strategic, unique, and developed on a case by case basis. As this is neither a good nor a bad thing, it simply implies that they beat to their own drum and find fulfillment in being completely in tune with who they are, internally. It also shows us that they proudly own the mystery behind their thoughts and personalized views towards life as a whole.

Living outside of the box of normalcy, these uncommon individuals are a rare breed and are oftentimes misunderstood and occasionally labeled as "the Others."

Chapter 1

The Others: Who Are They, Exactly?

"The Others" are people that see life beyond the normal ways of thinking. A rare breed, they are a combination of every type of individual you can imagine. Composed of intellects from all over the world. "The Others" can encompass individuals from all cultures, backgrounds, and walks of life. They are not biased to gender, social status, or class. They can be found anywhere, on any type of platform that paves the way for indifference, or any type of opposition as it pertains to worldly, psychological, and even emotional views.

Whether it be the suburbs, the projects, the White House, or even corporate America, you can come across an Other anywhere.

"The Others" are typically perceived by those who don't consider themselves as *the others* as "different." With aspects that set them apart from other individuals, they unapologetically but very humbly, beat to their own drum. Rather than having logical explanations as to why they do certain things, their actions are oftentimes driven by sane belief. The Others simply do what they feel and are firm followers of their own personal revelations, epiphanies, and instinctual segments. Others will proceed to carry out the concepts of any matter, idea, or way of living that rings true in their hearts and ignites their spiritual fire. Driven by purpose and passion, they go for the matters of life that give them a sensation similar to a gravitational pull.

The Others are known to have brilliant minds that birth some of the most unimaginable and one of a kind things. Through their unpredictable yet thought provoking perspectives, they challenge us to think outside of the box. Many of them have even been known to embark on world-changing journeys initiated by their own reflections and discoveries. Some of the world's most prominent and influential leaders are Others. Through their unwavering individuality, they have paved the way for trail blazers of the new era to follow their natural instincts in the pursuit of purpose and life altering endeavors.

Holding the will to inspire the world and evoke a sense of change in normal, everyday living, some of these Others can be easily identified throughout the past centuries as well as in the present day. Examples of some paths that Others have embarked on include but are not limited to social activism, creative artistry in any form, engineering and biological sciences, technological developments, higher education, and even motivational speaking.

By general conscious, The Others usually consider themselves as social outcasts. They tend to stay to themselves, and because they are occasionally misunderstood by many, they may not always be found in large circles. Others are aware that their mind frame is different, and they understand that it takes another rare mind to fully comprehend the depths of who they are. The Others are unmoved by the consumption of worldly opinions and social norms. As self assured individuals, they do not seek validation from others and they are also not too keen on the need to constantly be in close contact with other people. Because of this, Others do not force the presence or company of prospective peers, as they believe in the authenticity of relationships.

While the Others do have some qualities that may closely mirror those of normal everyday individuals, some of them are rather distinct and solely unique to their classification. Because some of their qualities can be perceived as common, how can we easily recognize The Others when we encounter them? Well, the truth is that we really can't.

Because everyone has a unique perception, the interpretation of "The Others" falls on the eye of the beholder. Upon encountering various individuals, what we can do, instead, is assess the things they do and say that challenge us to explore the depths of our mind. This is how we can easily identify and recognize who may be an Other versus who is not. Others challenge us to explore parts of our mind that either have not been exercised or disciplined in some way, shape or form. They lead us to ask probing questions which ultimately lead to us either identifying or tapping into our purpose.

Do we feel inspired? Do we feel more motivated? Have we become more driven? Are we suddenly compelled to do a thing that feels bigger than who we are? Are we adopting new ways of thinking and living? Are we disposing of old ways and habits that were once detriments to our growth? Do we feel moved? Whether we agree or disagree with the disposition at hand, do we feel challenged in some type of way? Are we persuaded? Perplex? Questioning of our own life strategies?

All questions posed the perfect examples of the types of things that happen, internally, when we encounter and interact with Others. Others Will always influence, challenge, or spark our curiosity in some way that makes us want to explore higher and deeper levels of consciousness and life, as a whole.

Chapter 2
Perception

Others are known to have "extreme levels of thinking." With their enlightening dispositions, they are usually very meticulous and sometimes even abstract with their words. Their intellectual authenticity classifies them as "different" in the eyes of those who would consider themselves "normal."

Think of the most radical, nonconforming, profound, or even analytical individuals you have come across. Do you think they may be Others? If you immediately identified them as "different" upon your first encounter, then they, most likely, are others. Perhaps you may even be an Other, yourself. This is also something to ponder. But despite this, the real question to consider is: what really classifies someone as "different?" Are the "normal," non-extreme thinkers different? Or are *the Others* different? Truthfully, it all depends on the nature of one's perception.

Perception is the realization or understanding of the world around us. When one perceives a person or object, their mind creates stereotypical or non-stereotypical ideas based on what is presented to them. Stereotypical ideas are created from prior knowledge about what one may perceive as similar or relatable. Non-stereotypical ideas are created when one has an open mind to the perception of things, whether experienced or not. Non-stereotypical perceptions are objective, and leave no room for a "positive" or "negative" bias to be made.

The Others are rather instinctive when it comes to maintaining non-stereotypical perceptions of the world. They are open-minded to other opinions and unclassified standpoints, which can be a great thing. Their consideration of the abnormal challenges us to look at life from an exploratory, rather than a confined lens.

Let's look at an example of a hardworking and goal-driven citizen. This person does a great job providing for his or her family, all while handling adult responsibilities. One may automatically perceive them as the type of individual who has it all together; the type of person who makes adulting look easy. However, when this person is in his or her room staring at four walls in solitude, what cycles through their mind? Can we assume that their mind is filled with "adult thoughts" such as parenthood and making ends meet? We may never know. Only that individual has the true answer to what's occurring in his or her mind.

Whether the thoughts are truthfully discussed or not is an even larger mystery. How can we determine if this person's true perception of the world has ever been revealed? How do we not know if this person is fed up with all that is happening in his or her world? Could it be stress? Fatigue? The truth is, we may never know, and that is the unambiguous beauty of perception.

Through the realm of perception, a person's mind has more power than he or she can ever imagine. This is because perception widens the road of potential outcomes and ideologies. In the example provided, we never came to a conclusion on what ran through this hard working citizen's mind. While some guesses may seem more logical than others, in reality, there is no real logical answer. because there is no logical answer. Unless we hear directly from the individual, perception leaves everything up to our imagination and the way we view life. In this case, there can never be a *right* or *wrong* way to view things, as the essence of individuality reigns supreme.

This is exactly how The Others approach life and the many people that they encounter. While they are known to accept people and things at face value, they are not known to interpret the behavior and reactions of others using the face value details, alone. Others believe that there are layers to everything in life, and they believe that perception is both broad and deep.

The Others believe that the road of perception is endless and that it oftentimes entails no concrete answers. The others correlate perception with vague and abstract principles that are merely solidified on an individual, case by case basis. As opposed to completely categorizing particular scenarios of life as "black" or "white," Others find a thrill in exploring the great areas of all that life has to offer. This includes but is not limited to learning and mastering the mind's personal experiences and perceptions of other people throughout individualized scenarios.

Chapter 3
Inner Turmoil

While The Others maintain a neutral outlook in their perception of human beings, they do not always experience this approach on the receiving end. Although they are highly esteemed for staying true to themselves, they sometimes struggle with feelings of isolation and misunderstanding. The Others rarely feel insecure or uncertain in how they feel. However, from time to time, they do tend to feel lonely and often question if there are other individuals, or other Others, who can truly attain a sense of who they are.

To the contrary, while they do face the inner turmoil of being set apart, they know that resistance in any form, typically comes from those who do not fall within their same classification, on a mental spectrum. Others, although not too fond of these moments, do not always allow the individuals to disrupt their energy. In fact, they mostly resort to fighting themselves within as they try to decipher, themselves, the reasons as to why they are occasionally misunderstood.

There's another category of "The Others" perceived by those who feel like they are not The Others. These individuals are the *other* "Others" who feel as if they are the commoners in society. They live cookie-cutter lifestyles and they believe their way of doing things is the most acceptable and appropriate way. While they are not necessarily perfectionists, they are loyal to conformity and are accustomed to the way things have always been. On occasion, they might even classify themselves as *different,* which is, indeed, a primary attribute of The Others in our context. These Others, the commoners, believe that their differentiation comes from living the routine, straight and narrow lifestyles. While they play it safe, The Others do not.

The Others are innovative risk takers who get a thrill from utilizing the *glass-half-full* perspective. They look to the optimistic endeavors of life and pursue anything that gives them momentum and they live for rewarding and fulfilling things that bring them joy. But unfortunately, there can be a downside to this when they are placed in the same environments as commoners. They can find themselves weighed down by a series of unsolicited remarks, opinions, and even questions that can either claim the title of curiosity or ridicule, depending on the personality of the individual in opposition.

When The Others merge paths with commoners, or *self-proclaimed Others*, an internal battle arises. While they still manage to confidently project their levels of self-assurance, they internalize conflicting feelings as they attempt to understand the world outside of them. To The Others, the ways and methods of commoners are concerning, and the feelings are quite mutual on the commoners' end. While The Others feel that commoners settle for less, commoners feel that The Others may be irrational in their pursuit of adventure.

In their lack of understanding, commoners can sometimes revert to extreme ridiculing or interrogation (intentional and unintentional) when they do not agree with what The Others are doing. They can even take on the form of high school and middle school students through their tantalizing and childlike behavior, which they occasionally mislabel as their inability to comprehend anything that does not suit their own preferences and values. This, in turn, causes

The Others to feel conflicted, ultimately asking themselves questions such as "Is something wrong with *me*?" or How am *I* not normal?" or "What makes *me* so different from *them*?" While these back and forth moments of questioning and self doubt may not last for long periods of time, the Others do tend to face these constant battles whenever they feel even an ounce of intellectual oppression and fatigue.

Despite this, in their overall analysis of self, The Others have learned to accept and understand the fact that not everyone is the same. Therefore, while they may experience disappointments at the reality of commoners failing to understand their levels of thinking, they do know that ultimately, the matters merely are telling of insecurities in the hearts of those commoners, as opposed to inadequacies of their own. With this in mind, they remain open, respectful and when necessary, adaptable to the inevitable reality of personal differences. However, to protect their energy, they are certain to not allow these types of individuals to invade spaces in their hearts and minds without permission. This is also why Others tend to be extremely discerning and reserved when it comes to the new development of close bonds and relationships.

Chapter 4
Relationships

The Others have an interesting way of building and maintaining relationships. Rather than diving in head first, they allow connections to form organically. They build relationships at their own pace, as they must be able to thoroughly read a person before exploring vulnerable territories.

The Others take pride in their sense of individuality and they appreciate being independent. When pursuing companionship with other human beings, they are very careful not to cross the lines of codependency in any way. Not only does this enable their comfort in solitude, but it also allows them to imagine living a joyous life without certain individuals in it.

While they may be a bit more distinctive in their approach towards new acquaintances, The Others do not follow this logic when it comes to close family members. To an Other, the love for a close family member is vastly powerful, in comparison to the love for a person who is not blood related. Others may find it easy to open up and let their guards down with family members. This is because familial bonds are typically established in the early stages of their lives, while most friendships, business partnerships, and romantic interests are developed over the course of time.

While we all have a sense of instinct and awareness of certain types of people, an Other's ability to "figure people out" is on a level of extremity. When meeting people for the first time, Others can judge an individual's actions and body language to determine whether someone is trustworthy or not. The Other also picks up on characteristics in attentiveness in physical conversations to draw conclusions about a person's true intentions. Although there is really no in-depth analysis that officially determines how attentive someone may be, an Other can comprehend the signs that show whether or not a person genuinely wants to communicate or associate with the individuals in their presence. This is typically how Others begin to know who they wish to have as acquaintances and who they desire to build friendships with.

An Other can pick up on the energy conveyed even when he or she is not in the physical presence of another human being. For instance, an Other can read a message and identify the true emotions that the composer may have toward a particular situation or circumstance, whether enthused or unenthused. While this is also a natural instinct of theirs, it enhances overtime as they become closer with specific individuals. With this intuitive ability, Others an easily determine the best actions to take if a decision needs to be made, and he or she can determine the best response to give. Additionally, this internal instinct especially comes in handy for an Other in the pursuit or maintenance of a romantic relationship or a business partnership. This relational component allows an Other to discuss and sometimes even combat significant matters in the most tactful way.

When navigating their relationships, Others make certain that they are never too entangled in one emotion. With an awareness of the inconsistency that emotions may bring, Others avoid placing emotional labels on themselves and on other people. While they have a keen understanding of emotional variations, they do believe in pure authenticity, across the board. For example, while they may portray happiness one day, they can be completely neutral the next day, which would not be abnormal to them. Others believe that an over portrayal of the happy emotion would be both exhausting and unrealistic. They believe that it would cause people to become accustomed to one particular side of them that may not reflect who they are as a whole, on every occasion. Because of this, Others believe that having and showing a proper balance is the best safety precaution, as it reduces the likelihood of them feeling pressured to compromise their emotions to the acceptance of other people.

Another safety precaution for Others is their ability to control emotional desires. Too many times, we as human beings, tend to act on what we strongly feel or think is best for us at the time, especially when it comes to forming relationships. Sometimes, we can actually be wrong but if we are too entangled in a person, situation or anything besides religious inquiries, we can steer ourselves away from personal goals. Others believe that acting in this nature is far from one who accomplishes great things in life, which is why they are very selective about who they reveal their emotions to and who they decide to form relationships with.

There are specific times where Others may need to be selective, yet strategic in their display of emotions. One of the most prominent examples of this is shown in the way an Other conducts him or herself while on a job. When getting to know colleagues, Others may openly express happiness and appeal to the concerns of other people in order to gain admiration and respect. While this may seem like a manipulative tactic, it is not. In reality, the Other is simply "playing it safe" to make sure he or she is not being manipulated. Once the Other is sure of the intent and recognizes sincerity amongst particular individuals or groups of people, he or she can act accordingly and give the individual some type of trust to a certain extent without completely letting his or her guard down.

Others know how to properly place the people in their lives, and if some belong in the past, Others believe in keeping it that way. Looking toward the future at all times, Others are not fond of inviting people from the past back into their lives. While Others do not believe in grudges and vengeful living, they do value letting go of past relationships that no longer serve them. The Others believe that dwelling in the past and trying to recreate past events will only keep them stuck and unhappy.

Others know how to maintain the mentality that "life goes on." He or she knows when to discontinue effort toward a situation and how to continue to live his or her life in the best way he or she knows how. The other's discontinued efforts save him or her from pondering over what's not meant to be. When an individual ponders over situations and tries to figure out a motive of why another individual acted as he or she did when there's a minor situation at hand, the other would describe this individual as wasting mental effort. Instead, the other feels that the individual could use this effort to strive to improve his or her code of life.

This individual could harness the knowledge he or she learned from a mistake in the past and know not to make the same mistake twice. Others feel that it only takes one time to make a mistake or to give an individual an inch of trust in order to determine the next step. They also feel that if and when mistakes are made, there is always beauty in the outcome. Others look to mistakes as opportunities to become more defined and equipped to handle the challenges that await them in the future. They feel that this perception of mistakes will allow them to lead more happier and productive lives.

The Others believe that as time continues to move on, we all should follow suit. Through this motto, they believe that we will all be able to experience more meaningful and fulfilling lives.

Chapter 5
Social Settings

While in social settings, The Others do not immediately reveal their full personality. Similar to the ways in which they assess others on a relationship scale, they must also go through the same observational methods in social settings. Others do not believe in unveiling their strong emotions entirely. They believe that neutrality is the best emotion to begin with and they use their wisdom to decide whether their participation in a social event is necessary or not.

Others prefer to get a feel for the people and the atmosphere beforehand. Once they do decide to participate and tap into the general characteristics of those who they are interacting with, they adjust little by little. They typically do this by picking up on the flow of conversations and mirroring small segments of whatever emotion is being portrayed (happiness, sadness, anger, or sorrow) towards the situation is at hand. Others do this when they are comfortable with engagement, however they still have a way of participating without fully divulging all of their own emotions.

Others value concealment as a primary principle. Taking pride in the mystery of discretion, they believe that everyone should know how to effectively conceal their emotions in favorable situations. While Others conceal their own personal information, they do not keep a closed ear when it comes to the personal information of others. They are both open minded and receptive, especially if someone needs a listening ear. Additionally, they also find value in any outside information they receive, as it helps them to draw conclusions on the personal character traits of others. For example, information provided could give Others insight on how an individual would react in certain situations, and how reliable he or she would be in regards to doing favors and performing vital tasks.

Although vigilant and observant, Others still know how to have a good time while socializing. However, their ability to display full-on enjoyment depends on the types of individuals that are present. Others are aware of those who act as parasites toward their actions and thoughts. They know that these types of people can be quite manipulative in social settings, so therefore, if they choose to exhibit neutrality as opposed to enjoyment, they are simply keeping themselves safe from emotional scorn.

In the midst of their neutrality, Others can still manage to participate in conversations. As opposed to shutting down completely, they base their conversational participation on their perception of the other individuals. They do this by carefully choosing their words and being selective with what they share, in order to prevent the wrong information from getting to the wrong person.

Others know how to avoid troublesome situations at all cost and are always ejective to peer pressure. In their opinion, peer pressure gives them a sense of collaboration in a group scene, and this is not what they strive to obtain. If and when the Others come in contact with those who decide not to use good judgment in social settings, their sense of individualism illuminates above all else, and they know just what to do to not get involved in any poor decision making activities.

Others believe that adaptability is the key to human companionship. With this in mind, they know how to conduct themselves by changing their persona, where applicable, in social situations. Whether they are surrounded by complete strangers or people that may be privy to particular sides of them, they know how to maintain a good social balance while still staying true to themselves. For example, if an Other is conducting a conversation with two different friends who have him or her as a common connection, the Other will use a conversational approach that caters to all parties. The Other will not reveal inside information, subliminal messages, or even humorous gestures that may only be relevant to one of the friends. Instead, he or she will find and focus on aspects that both companions can relate to.

When conversing in social environments, an Other is not easily persuaded by the opinions and perspectives of everyone else. Because of many external influences from other people, an Other does not want to unconsciously be persuaded by how other people present themselves to the world. Sometimes, an Other may take in a few partial lessons from different people and use them to gather his or her own interpretation. While he or she may occasionally follow the logic of human beings, an Other ultimately takes pride in the ability to think for him or herself. An Other knows that his or her personality is shaped by a unique recollection of morals, thoughts and ways of living. Because of this, an Other knows what to take in and process as wisdom and what to take in and process as waste disposal.

Others find that their greatest success in social settings stems from their ability to recharge during selective times of the day. They do this by taking some time alone to reflect and release the components of their mind. For Others, time spent in isolation paves the way for independence, self development and cognitive sharpening. Through alone time, Others are able to connect with themselves while remaining in tune with their own personal ethics and codes of life. Others believe that solitude is an essential part of life that should be incorporated in everyone's day. They epitomize it as the key to self-government and a greater sense of intelligence and stability. The Others believe that those who spend a great amount of time around large groups of people (and little to no time alone) may possibly be experiencing an identity crisis or some type of internal discomfort.

Because Others spend so much time recharging their minds, they are known to always think ahead of the game in social settings. Before stepping foot into any room or atmosphere, they have most likely played out several scenarios in their minds, followed by potential outcomes and repercussions. The Others believe that this type of preparation in social settings keeps them on their toes, and they also see it as a preventative measure when it comes to handling conflict.

Chapter 6
Conflict

Others believe that social matters are typically driven by the strong emergence and spread of common emotions. Whether these social matters are informal and robust, or formal and regulatory, Others believe that there are shared emotions among the individuals who unite themselves for the sake of such causes. Others believe these causes can be driven by a number of emotions that surround personal, social, and even political matters that people tend to feel passionate about. The emotions, whether positive, negative or vague, are not the primary point of concern in the Others' assessment of a matter.

However, Others do understand that the commonality of emotions is what fuels the power behind a particular cause, movement or scenario. Supportive of the dynamics of integration, relationship building and even networking where applicable, Others find this idea of shared emotions to be quite remarkable. The only time Others find themselves being reluctant to the idea of shared emotions is when those emotions serve as the foundation of a rising conflict.

While Others do believe in and value the unison of like minds, they understand that life, through its inevitability, will present moments where conflict may arise. With a thorough understanding that everyone has their own unique views and perspectives as pertained to emotional development and intellect, the Others especially find this reality to be a true component of conflict. Others define conflict as anything that opposes the flow of harmony and they also believe that the root cause of conflict stems from differentiating emotions, along with misaligned values and perceptions.

Others are aware that emotional differences tend to cause outbursts of sensitivity, rage and even resentment among groups of people who refuse to accept the personal standpoints of one another. Others also understand that there is a high sense of emotional maturity required in order to effectively avoid and confront conflict, especially when expressing their own personal views to those who are not classified as "Others."

Others are aware of their own emotional strengths, and they are also aware that there will be people who oppose their points of view and ways of living. As opposed to being angry and offended, Others believe that a simple suppression of their own emotions may possibly be the most effective strategy for resolving conflict. Others have a thorough understanding of the strength of their own emotion, thoughts and feelings. When they feel strongly about something they have no problem being open and transparent. but while they are confident in their own emotions define suppression to be the best form of resistance to conflict because they already know that many people will not understand their level of thinking. Others are not perfect and due to their emotional differences they have often found themselves in a number of conflicts especially throughout the early years of their life. Because of this, they find beauty in reflection and learning from past mistakes in order to navigate and successfully resolve their way out of conflicting situations.

Another strategy that others use to avoid conflict is to place scenarios over and over in their mind. Whether these scenarios have taken place in the past or not at all, Others believe that this tactic sharpens their emotional and mental capacity and allows them to remain calm, proactive, resourceful, and prepared in the face of conflict. Subconsciously, Others are also replaying scenarios in their minds to obtain a full understanding of various matters that may have already occurred, or have the possibility of taking place again. They do this all throughout the day, no matter where they are as it helps them to make the most appropriate decisions in the face of complicated matters.

Even though this ability could be a nuisance to the average person's emotional well-being, because the other has the ability to suppress his or her emotions, he or she knows how to feel a sense of mental apathy from analyzing situations from every angle. Their ability to form a mental apathy toward making decisions gives them an advantage, as pertained to their capacity to live life with no regrets. This ability serves as one of the primary reasons why they are able to maintain success throughout multiple areas of their lives.

In simpler terms, Others fully understand when to turn specific emotions on, and when to turn them off. They know that regardless of how they may feel towards a matter on the inside, they can neither control nor alter the way other individuals interpret, receive, and respond to certain things.

Chapter 7
Motivation & Aspirations

All Others have or are working toward primary goals. In the process of achieving their goals, Others do everything in their will power to ensure that their work is efficient and far above levels of satisfaction. Committed to the mission at hand, they try to not let idleness interfere with their work. Others have the discipline to stay focused on a task until it is completed and do not allow external distractions to halt their progress. Others believe in planning and strategizing their course of actions when carrying out major tasks. To maintain focus and a clear mind, they typically go into stages of isolation to ensure that their levels of concentration are not compromised. Once Others have their hearts set on something, they do whatever it takes to be successful, no matter how long the process may be. Others have no problem adhering to tight deadlines. While working towards their goals, they value time as an essential and limited component to their success.

Others know the difference between individuality and pride, which allows them to be confident in knowing exactly what they are capable of achieving and what they are not. Others believe in being humble and resourceful at all times. In the event that they need assistance, they are not too afraid to speak up and ask for help. Others do not dwell on their mistakes, and they also do not pinpoint the mistakes of others. Instead, they focus on the vital lessons and use them as guides to do better, moving forward.

Others do not let the capacity of other individuals dictate their own mental capacity. They understand that the inability of someone else neither correlates nor aligns with their own ability to give something a try and succeed at it. They also do not allow naysayers to get in their way as they strive to accomplish goals. They are aware that while some individuals may vocalize negative opinions due to their own incapabilities, others may simply not want to see them succeed. Others use this logic as motivation to continue on their path towards success and to go above and beyond the naysayers' attempts. Others do not settle for what other people have to express about an experience unless it's absolutely wise and logical.

Others set short-term and long-term goals for themselves. As an example, short-term goals, for Others, can concern daily life tasks relative to their current positions in life. Long-term goals can cater to their visionary sides and reach far into the future as pertained to positions or things they wish to obtain later on in life. Their short-term goals may or may not intertwine with their long-term goals. One example of this intertwining entails an Other focusing on being successful in college. On the other hand, an instance where short term and long term goals do not align consists of an Other remembering to take out their trash on the neighborhood "trash day."

Others take direct advantage of the opportunities placed before them on the table of life. When contemplating decisions and particular journeys to embark upon, they only ponder over situations that will have a severe detrimental effect on their future. Others do not place too much effort into the decision making process when small decisions are at hand. Oftentimes, they feel as though too much pondering over small tasks limits their focus, mental capacity and performance towards larger tasks.

Others believe that while small tasks are important, having a multitude of small tasks in comparison to larger tasks, leads to an insignificant life. Others think of small tasks as typical routines, such as eating one's favorite foods or watching one's favorite shows. Others perceive smaller tasks as simple, and occasional leisure activities that do not jeopardize the well-being of the performer or those around the performer. To the contrary, they define large tasks as those that jeopardize the well-being of the performer or those around the performer. Others believe that large tasks challenge us and sharpen our set of skills. They believe that the key to productivity is to have many large tasks readily available to commit to.

Others are always thinking outside of the box and they know how to become masters of their universe. While they are concerned with all that they are destined to achieve in the primary realm, they are certain to not let their secondary goals fall by the wayside. They believe in prioritizing and coming up with master plans that allow them to divide and categorize their goals effectively. Master plans also give Others a sense of supremacy that eliminates constant worrying, stress, and anxiety. With master plans, Others can freely devote time to scheduling other activities of their lives without feeling too overwhelmed.

Others can often become trapped in their own thoughts when trying to achieve their goals. While this can temporarily stifle them, it does not do so for long. Others may take a long time to ponder over the best action to take for a task, but when finally devising a strategy to accomplish a major goal, they do so full-fletched and wholeheartedly. Others are aware that because their own thoughts help them get out of troublesome mental situations, they can channel the same energy, aggression and relentlessness within to push themselves forward.

When it comes to aspirations and matters of the heart, Others have an abstract and oftentimes incomprehensible mind. They know how to look deeper into certain things people normally wouldn't consider at all. They can take the rarest components and processes and somehow connect them to make them make sense. This sense of ambiguity can work to their advantage not just in their execution of work related tasks, but also in their aspiration and pursuit of creativity. A great example of this is demonstrated in their analysis of music. Others can relate to, analyze, and correlate particular emotions from a variety of musical sources. The sources can include characters in a video game, a scene from a television show, a playlist in their favorite retail store, or even the radio. Using these sources, Others can pick up on similarities between perceived morals, feelings, moods, and find ways to channel inner feelings of familiarity. For Others, feeling a sense of connection between sound effects causes them to feel more in tune with their own aspirations and creative abilities.

Chapter 8
Creativity

Others know how to evoke energy through their productions. Productions allow them to feel fueled. motivated, persistent, and in control of their own destiny. Productions, to Others, consist of anything unique, special, and innovative.

Others classify productions as the result of them taking the personal time to explore who they are while further tapping into the depths of their own souls. While a production does not necessarily constitute a song, it could for an Other who is musically inclined.

For example, as it pertains to song production, Others could use their communication abilities to evoke strong energy and emotions within another person. Through various words, instruments and even a combination of sounds, musically inclined Others can not only speak directly to the minds of other people, but they can also reveal the components of their very own minds in just a short amount of time. For all Others, whether musically inclined or not, communication can tie in anything verbal, technical, and subliminal carried throughout the messages depicted in their creative works. These can also include paintings, poems, books, and other creative based avenues used to transmit energy and suppressed emotions.

Once Others are able to evoke energy through their productions, they have the ability to persuade the emotions of those who pay close attention to their logic. Then, through the publicizing of this shared logic, universal connections are formed with various people from a wide range of demographics. This is typically how the world's most creative geniuses of Others have gained their following and landed a global influence. Their ability to attract mass audiences through their own logic ignited an emotional familiarity that several people could personally relate to.

Others believe that the mere act of evoking energy through creativity always has a specific reason tied to it. Because creative energy tends to be so strong in the eyes of an Other, they believe that the transfer of energy, in any form by an Other, can be freely marketed strictly on the basis of how it makes people feel. Furthermore, Others also believe that the evoking, in itself, does not serve as a host for positive or negative energy but merely as a platform of expansion for whatever it is that the creative "artists" wants his or her target audience to feel. Others believe that the positive and negative energy classifications are created only on the basis of personal outlooks and interpretations of occurrences in an individual's fluctuating life.

As an instance, let's say that one is having a tremendous day and decides to listen to elastic music in order to heighten his or her euphoric state. This individual is going to be feeding off the energy of the music along with the already positive energy that exists from the circumstances of what's happened in the course of the day. On the contrary, let's take it that one is having a gloomy day and decides to listen to music that's typically described by the general population as emotive. The person described in this scenario is feeding off the negative energy of the music along with the already negative energy that exists from the circumstances of his or her day.

In extreme cases, while it may appear that the elastic music generated good energy, and the "emo" music generated bad energy, some may not agree with either one of these perspectives. Some may feel that both genres emit negative energy, especially if they were never accustomed to listening to music in those categories. Some may find these genres to be components of evil, and psychopathological thought processes, as opposed to mere expressions of joy or sadness. Other individuals may find themselves either indifferent to or accepting of both for no reason some more serious than the other.

Through this example, Others teach us the power of energy transfer through individualization and creativity. They also encourage us to acknowledge the significance of not being judgmental when it comes to the creative and energy outlet sources utilized by other people. The Others show us that while there is no automatic classification on good versus bad energy, the personal things that we experience and feel are the very components that categorize them as such. These are also the same components that depict the particular paths we choose to take when it comes to exploring our creative outlets.

As pertained to the depths of creativity, Others simply believe that the emission of good or bad energy first starts within the mind before it is connected with a reason or label. This is why some creative and talented individuals of our present day may be accepted, and the same reasons why some of them may be not. Similar to their own concepts of perception, Others feel that creativity and the evoking of energy are also in the eyes of the beholder.

Chapter 9

Humanitarian Endeavors

Others believe that we are not to remain dependent on particular moments and events in life. With the awareness that uncertainty is inevitable, they believe that we should live each day with the understanding that not every day is promised. While they do believe in predicting probability, they know that there is never a sure way to determine the outcome of an event.

For Others, this thought process is carried over into every area of their lives. They especially use it as a driving force to sew positive seeds into the world whenever they can. Others feel that while they cannot control the ups and downs of everyday life, they *can* control the ways in which they choose to make it better while they are here. For Others, making life better involves anything purpose-driven; anything that allows them to step outside of themselves. Another way to put this is simply, anything that allows them to serve and give back to their community while being influential. They usually come across these opportunities by first tapping in to the very things that bring them joy on a regular basis. For example, some may start with special hobbies or activities, such as teaching, or painting, etc. They then look for ways to merge the things they love with their capacity to extend support and helping hands to other people.

Others feel good when they can contribute to a higher purpose or charitable cause. With this enlightenment, they are often led to participate in a variety of movements, activities, and ventures geared towards the betterment of humanity and even the environment. Collectively, Others have a wide variety of interests and passions. Unlimited by a singular focus, their humanitarian efforts can cater to people of all ages, backgrounds, and walks of life.

Others believe that we should all strive to perceive and reciprocate things in a positive way, no matter where we are in our lives. Even though we cannot avoid the unexplainable and incomprehensible at times, we should do everything in our power to do what is "just" according to lawful and ethical standards, even if that means leaving our own bubbles to do so. Others believe that our innate gifts are to be used not just for our own personal advancement, but for the enhanced wellness of others. They encourage us to utilize our creativity and brilliant minds to find life changing solutions to social problems.

For Others, giving, in any type of way, serves as a foundation for true, wealthy living. In this case, *wealth,* to Others, would epitomize spiritual fullness, or satisfaction of the heart as a result of extended kindness. Others feel accomplished when they are able to add something of value to the lives and circumstances of other individuals. While they may not be extreme seekers of public accolades, they enjoy moments where they have been able to meet needs and even offer words of encouragement. Others are able to clearly recognize when they have influenced a person or a group of people's perspective on life in a positive manner. While they may not always be immediately conscious of the levels of adoration received, they can always recognize and appreciate the imitated words and actions of the individuals that they have influenced.

While Others love to give and be of influence, they also like to join forces with other individuals who share similar values, mindsets, and a passion for similar causes. Others are especially excited when they discover that the recipients of their inspiration includes children, emerging leaders of subsequent generations, and even seasoned intellects of the eras before them.

Finding value in the unapologetic authenticity of the new generations, Others have developed a deep sense of love, appreciation, and respect for the revelation of truth brought about by the generations long before them. Because of these aspects, Others remain ready and willing to support these change provoking leaders. Internally looking to them as "Others" in and of themselves, Others believe that individuals of these groups serve as the gateways and catalysts for change, innovation, new fulfillment, and advancement in any way, shape, or form.

Chapter 10
Spirituality & Religion

When it comes to purpose, impact, and legacy, an Other wishes to be memorialized by a solid foundation of individual philosophy. He or she would not approve of being compared to another person. Instead, he or she would rather be commemorated for advanced levels of influence that came directly from the power and guidance of a Higher Power, as opposed to a particular individual.

An Other has the mentality of a leader and not a follower. Through the desire to set him or herself apart, the Other believes that leadership paves the way for legacy, as it provokes one to look to internal values as opposed to the external influence of the world. An Other believes that looking inward serves as a gateway to spiritual connection, advancement and even provision.

Holding firmly to their own interpretations and beliefs, Others, as a whole, do not allow other human beings to determine how they choose to acknowledge, respond to, or connect with a deity or deities. While they can listen to other individuals share information or interpreted meanings on particular aspects of a deity, or deities, Others base the truths on their own abilities to formulate original thoughts and ideas to the best of their knowledge. Though there may be external philosophies that Others utilize when creating the foundation for their own spiritual or religious logic, they ultimately establish their own new philosophy from the combination of the external philosophies.

If an Other has external influences, he or she may only admit to being influenced by particular characteristics of influential individuals and not the individual as a whole. Because of this mentality, the other knows that the only way he or she is going to stand as an originator alone is to not fully admire another human being. An Other would appreciate the fact that one's understanding of their own philosophical authenticity indicates that he or she recognizes the Other for accomplishing the goal of creating the philosophy. In the event that there is an understanding barrier between an Other's philosophy and the audience of followers, the Other remains devoted to improving the message. Rather than feeling like a failure due to the misunderstanding of the audience, the Other, instead, puts great effort into effectively communicating the message so that it becomes easily comprehensible across all platforms. In doing this, the Other is sure to limit confusion but is also careful not to change the context of the message or any of its key points.

While the Other does view the world as a feeding ground for knowledge, he or she will never compromise ideas and beliefs to serve the general public. As an advocate for individualism, the Other stands true to self and knows how and when to conserve his or her thoughts accordingly. He or she also believes that the primary focus of logic and individualism is to not be affected by the general public's annoyances. What strengthens an Other's ability to stand so firm in this is his or her submission to a Higher Power.

Others have the capacity to maintain their individuality and focus because they know how to surrender to what is above them. Through every component of their lives, they know that their strength comes from a Deity with far more strength, power, and wisdom than they can ever imagine. Others live by faith and are only moved and shaken up by things if their High Power deems it necessary. Others do not try to understand the incomprehensible if they are bound by spiritual beliefs. They allow their Deity to control their fate, if one exists in their lives. While some of them may bind themselves to religious customs, some of them simply choose to incorporate better belief methods into their everyday lives. Collectively, they all try to practice living worry-free lifestyles, and through their faith, they are able to find rest in the fact that some type of progress is being made, which then allows them to better understand why particular events have occurred throughout their lives.

There may be times when Others are not quite sure of the reasons why something spanned out the way it did. Although they pride themselves on their individual philosophy, they also understand that some things will always be a mystery to them. An example of this can apply to Others looking for closure from particular situations or individuals, or even clarity on particular paths to take in their lives. In cases like this, Others do not rely on their individual philosophies completely. They turn directly to the principles of their Deity to see if there is a standard to comprehend and cope with the unknown. Others teach us that we can never fully rely on ourselves, and that is a good thing. They also show us that we should not be timid when it comes to exploring and taking advantage of our spiritual backgrounds, if we have them.

An Other relies on his or her Deity for guidance and wisdom, especially in the most critical areas of life. If change is to ever come, which it will, an Other knows that he or she must put effort into seeking spiritual counsel. This will then allow his or her choices to be measured by core values of the High Power, along with any spiritual beliefs that may have developed over time. If and when an Other may be considering long-term change in a situation, then he or she is sure to focus not only on improving present day practices, but also, altering decisions for the future with the goal of paving a path guided by spiritual beliefs.

Others understand that the core of who they are in life, and who they strive to become, stems from the incorporation of their own practices. While they do not believe in forcing their spiritual or religious methodologies on other people, they do believe that we should all be able to connect with a higher source, in efforts to be better and to live better. With this knowledge, they encourage us to take hold of our original beliefs while still managing to be contemporary in our interactions with society. Others believe that this will keep us adaptable and open-minded as we engage and form connections with other people. They also believe this strategy will allow us to communicate effectively, lead prosperous lives, and become more aware of who we are.

Chapter 11
Self-Awareness

Think of all of the types of Others you have come across that left a lasting impact on your life and personal perspective. Whether they were funny, reserved, too talkative, too quiet, intimidating, or not much of anything, we have all, in some way, been impacted by an Other.

Others spark an inner sensation within us that compels us to take leaps and strides of faith. Regardless of the specifics concerning how and in what ways we are moved, the mere presence, connection to, or conversation with an Other propels us to tap into our higher selves. While esteemed for their capacity to stand out in the rarest forms, Others challenge us not to be different, necessarily, but to be more self aware. Others believe that while distinctiveness sets us apart, self-awareness sets us free and ultimately propels us forward.

Through their surrendering to a High Power, Others have a higher sense of self-awareness and the ability to maintain stability throughout every area of their lives. Through their surrendering to a Higher Power, Others are filled with a lasting peace and confidence that cannot be shaken. By having a greater feeling of self-awareness, Others are aware that conformity with "non-Others" does not yield the ability to suppress human sensations. To ensure that they are maintaining strength in challenging areas of their lives, Others keep a strict moral code in order to achieve personal fulfillment and a sense of grand accountability. Others believe that anything outside of the realm of their personal progress, happiness, and development poses a threat to their sense of self-awareness. Careful to always remain in tune with who they are at the core, they believe that anything standing in opposition to self-awareness and elevation serves as a distraction from their primary goal. Because of this, they know how to channel internal disciplinary tactics in realms where challenges may be at an altitude.

Others know how to learn from past faults and experiences of normality. They look at their mistakes as opportunities to process knowledge, learn lessons, and gain wisdom as an advantage. Others believe that while their mistakes are lessons, they serve as keys to the essence of who they are and where their path will lead. While Others do everything in their power not to repeat common mistakes associated with ways of normality, they never shy away from acknowledging the valuable concepts learned.

Others believe that self-awareness entails an acknowledgement of all of the things that have contributed to their growth as well as the development of their character. While they are firm in their stance to dissociate from former ways of living, they do appreciate the opportunity to share their journey with others, in efforts to lead them down the right path. Others believe that self-awareness brings an automatic separation from those who are enslaved to normalized ways of thinking. While this can become rather uncomfortable from time to time, they acknowledge that conforming to normal tendencies will only cause them to fall under the labels of a mere conformist in society, which diminishes their sense of individuality as well as the love they worked so hard to establish from within.

Having an awareness of self allows Others to own who they are. It also gives them the capacity to maintain control of their emotions while combating negative feelings that are strongly evoked in particular situations. As an instance, Others could feel a sensation of anger or sorrow that is deeply heartfelt. While there is nothing wrong with the feeling, in itself, an Other understands that his or her response to the feeling is what illuminates the positive or negative outcome. As opposed to self isolating, or taking matters out on someone else, Others know that the way to get through unwanted feelings and emotions is to first allow them to flow. Through self-awareness, Others grant themselves the space to feel the sensations with maturity, and learn to wholeheartedly release them in a healthy way that does not affect their overall progress and advancement in life.

Others find it useless to dwell in any type of rage or internal hurt. Upon taking the time to heal and persist through the many things that life has thrown their way, Others realize that their strength is found in first acknowledging where they are in life. In doing so, they allow their Higher Power to take over in redefining and molding their minds while giving them the hope they need to move forward in life. Others teach us that self-awareness requires the daily practice of suppressing familiar and toxic emotions while trusting their Higher Power to replenish them with fresh, new and awakening vibrations. Others understand that emotional intelligence and suppression are keys to sustaining their faith when reality does not seem to align with their expectations. With a full surrender and internal acceptance in the avenue of self-awareness, Others are able to live happy lives free from bitterness and resentment.